the hook-switch goodbye

# the hook-switch goodbye

*Poems by Christine Brooks*

Turning Point

© 2023 by Christine Brooks

Published by Turning Point
P.O. Box 541106
Cincinnati, OH 45254-1106

ISBN: 9781625494504

Poetry Editor: Kevin Walzer
Business Editor: Lori Jareo
Cover art: Shannon Gallagher and Celina McMahon

Visit us on the web at www.turningpointbooks.com

## Dedication

To the sisterhood, who,
when I could no
longer walk
gathered 'round
and carried me through

# Table of Contents

awake.................................................................................9
order..................................................................................10
you died............................................................................11
fishing with corn..............................................................12
the ladder.........................................................................14
beyond..............................................................................15
paper bag butterflies......................................................16
Jericho...............................................................................18
the stone...........................................................................19
the mail.............................................................................20
the hook-switch goodbye..............................................22
64 days AC........................................................................24
the waves..........................................................................25
Lonely As..........................................................................27
the leaving........................................................................28
March................................................................................29
the holes...........................................................................31
the Ethels..........................................................................33

## awake

it's not that I wasn't tired
or slept with all the lights on
inside the house & out
and it isn't because Covid stole
your last breath
when
I couldn't be with you

    that keeps me awake

No,
it isn't any of those reasons
that has me awake through the long minutes of the
noiseless nights
   still weeks later

what keeps my eyes from closing
is the feeling I get in the moments just before
 waking
when I am both asleep & awake
a foot on each plane

the feeling that it was a bad dream
and
you did not die

but I wake to find you died
all over again

# order

I stood, winded from shoveling
long enough to notice the houses
across the narrow street   *his*
narrow street 7, 13, 17



I wondered for a minute

about     where     9, 11 and 15    were
but
   decided
           wherever they      were

had
     to  be
better
than
   where
                             I was

## you died

ten months after the world sheltered & isolated
days before the vaccine became available

tired
in pain
confused and alone
wishing harder to be with *her* than to be here,
    anymore

with the chance to call and say goodbye
meeting death head on as warriors do
unafraid of the valley because
paradise was waiting
—calling

or so you wanted to believe

you called
asking to come off the breathing machines
so, you could be on time for dinner with mom

    —and I was not invited

# fishing with corn

I remember fishing with my father not
in the way most would, at least
I don't think so

*No, don't hurt the worm*, I said *please*
don't hurt the worm
*it's okay,* he always said, even though
we both knew it wasn't
as he did his best to tie the worm in a knot
around my shiny hook instead of
piercing his small worm body
knowing that he would drown
anyway

we decided corn was safer

I wasn't the son he wanted if kids were even
in his dreams
and I certainly wasn't the fishing buddy
he could have had

but still

when we fished with corn
on the banks of a tiny pond in a small town
that no one ever heard of
and allowed ourselves to be small

like the corn niblet on my silver hook
we were
    — happy

## the ladder

she drips, crying
still for that last night
outside
when it was warmer than it
should have been for a
November night
and they sat outside, sipping cocktails
and changing floodlights
while they still could, before
the snow & darkness came

the broken-down wooden ladder
wobbly at best
had her closer to Heaven than she had been
 in so long
so long in fact that she forgot how it felt
to be up there with him holding
her, as rickety as it was
he held on tight as she stretched on tippy toes for the
    light

now his chair leans against the shed
    and the old ladder is back in the garage
and she sits alone    and the grand tree who had always
been alive
could do nothing
but weep
because she did not
understand

# beyond

sometimes I remember
wishing to live in a place
beyond the paneling

but then I remember that
I would live there too

## paper bag butterflies

I thought you were elegant
thoughtful, even a gentleman
and even more than that, I thought you were
a special kind of man

the kind of man that laughed & hugged & cared
when it mattered most in a time of desperation
& isolation
when the only face I saw was that of a poet
on my computer screen and
the man in the moon

you reached out, concerned more for my safety
than your own, but
perhaps because you believed that you were too mean
to catch a hoax,
so, comfort was easy for you

I believed even in the timing of meeting you,
and acted brave and put together so you wouldn't
hear me complain,
hear me sound needy
weak

but you weren't any of those things
you were no Monarch
you were what you had always been
a paper bag butterfly

floating on the dampness of a
March night

nothing more, nothing less

# Jericho

I was grateful to him, then
and still   for
visiting when no one else could
and for changing his name

because

a dream chose that and
he believed that dream and so
he became
the kind of person the kind of poet
the kind of believer
that without even knowing it
gives hope when there is none
because that's what words
and dreams and dreamers
do

# the stone

I have a bleached beach stone
that with enough whiskey and weed,
looks like a heart

so instead of punching
trashcans garage walls windows toolboxes
I hold that stone that fits so perfectly in my hand
it's hard to imagine the maker didn't carve it
   just for me

feel its coolness softness strength
I imagine the beach I found it on
and the wave that I must have caught
touching the stone to my face I remember
the burn on my cheeks
from sun and wind and frost
—probably

I can hold all of that, but I cannot punch
 when
the stone is in my hand

# the mail

I was on the front porch today
when the mailman came
he could not see me slouched
down low on the futon  and
we had no mail so
he had no reason to stop

I watched him
the only face we saw for so many
daysweeksmonths
the only order in our lives that
for reasons we did not understand
not completely anyway,
had been put on hold, frozen
shuttered sheltered quarantined

we got through those March days
with only each other, in the small
house on the loud street that I
cursed for its inability to be peaceful

just,
me and him
 and the mailman

tonight, I saw the
mailman across the street
walking fast trying, it seemed
to not look this way

but he did


as he made his way to #7
he glanced this way
and his face frowned so hard I
felt it deep
in my tummy, but

he did not pause, as he had so many times before
did not take a knee, as he had when I told him
you had Covid
and he did not cry, as he did
at your casket
because the mail
must go on

and that, well that,
 that
you would have loved.

## the hook-switch goodbye

I have hated talking on the telephone
 for years,
trust issues somehow the root
*they* all say

trusting that the caller would not talk
too long or yell too much or do
anything really
that makes me anxious or otherwise
uncomfortable I do what I must for
work, for life and to at least seem
normal

you never did
make phone calls hard
until that Thursday morning at
8:15 when you called to say
enough
you had had enough

so,
Hello
don't forget to let Clancy out
thank you
I love you

and that
was the last new memory
I would make of you

Goodbye

## 64 days AC

my world existed now in
three distinct sections

before you had Covid BC
during Covid DC
and after Covid
AC

a storm blew in sideways
tonight
tossing the leaves we didn't
rake because
a November night BC distracted us
with warm breezes, long stories
and cocktails

they would still be there
in the spring
we told each other

it didn't occur to us that
you
wouldn't

# the waves


you called from the hospital
the first night
sounding only mildly inconvenienced
 and asked when I was coming to get you

you were coming home, even the
doctor said so, that first night
so, I washed your sheets and made soup
since I was in quarantine it was
ala Brooksie, as you liked to call
my meals that had no recipe
only using ingredients, we already had
stone soup, sometimes but you
never complained, always saying
it's not bad or if you really liked it,
it was *different*
no matter what though, it was never
as good as,
    beans on toast

you didn't come home though, not
the next day or even, the
next
still, you sounded good, strong
even through the sound of the oxygen being forced
 into your tired body

sorry you have to miss work,
you said

let's go over the DNR,
they said


both repeating now
until they didn't

and everything went
flat

# Lonely As

I knew alone but   I never knew lonely
not in the way the broken-hearted sing
about it anyway

Until that Sunday morning when I woke to
the smell of the coffee,
that I remembered to make the night before &
 could pour before the timer
 went off and it was cold
—Again

and heavy bruised clouds covered your small
house on that street,
that street
that street that never went anywhere

And I made banana pancakes the way you used to
Like them with
chocolate chips and cinnamon
and extra extra syrup

As Sunday morning smells drifted out
to the sidewalk   even
the Hyacinth tipped their grape caps
 to the dining room windows    and I realized
I was as Lonely as a
March butterfly

# the leaving

they took you away
first the funeral home staff
from my arms
then your niece and nephews
with care and love
to the grave

on a stretcher
in a coffin

they took you away
unseens
unknowns
in a hearse, I imagine
from me when
I could not visit
could not hold

and then, I watched
them take your truck
more people who
did not know
could not know

the story of your
—life

# March

I've been thinking a lot about
March
last March
*that* March mostly

a time when we did not know
what was coming
because we weren't paying attention
and even if we were we
never
thought it could happen to us
would happen to us

but it was

coming for us
for the lives of over 3 million people
coming for us
for those that raised us
coming for us
without regard
without warning
without prejudice    mostly

just, coming for us

that March
the entire world closed its doors
and shuttered

and sheltered
and prayed
even the folks who didn't pray
   —prayed
we prayed for safety
we prayed for understanding
and we prayed for a time to open
our windows and our doors
and hug those we love
  again


and the things that we thought
mattered
did not seem to matter at all
and all that did matter was
the decision
to be a good human

and still, some
refused

# the holes

I saw the most beautiful
flowers tonight

in the moments    just before
the sun set
when it was still and bright
and hopeful   with
dreams of pinks and orange clouds
nearby

I saw them
   as if
they only existed for me and   even
police sirens, car alarms, and barking dogs
fell silent
as they curtsied and swayed

to

the breeze    in perfect
harmony with their host

magical white flowers high
atop the tall maple tree across
the street,
            danced

reminding me of the
   many times, that you

made me laugh and smile and feel
Happy when you danced with Mom
and
I almost forgot
   for a second

that I would never again chuckle as you
polka-ed your way around many
the dance floor
cheesing for the camera
in your suspenders and
suit pants rolled up to show off
your white socks

I watched, mesmerized,  as those
magical flowers
faded from white to pink
before my eyes

and I hoped I was sleeping,
because maybe, the sleeping me
didn't know

that maple trees do
   not    blossom
cannot    blossom

and the flowers
and the magic
were nothing more than
the spaces in between

# the Ethels

I made the call, text
really   to my Ethel
to say dad was not well,
he was Covid positive and things
and life looked
   dim


the Ethels had seen so much
poverty, loneliness, & abuse that we
decided long ago
that those events made us
more than friends
more than family
more than any word could mean   so
we became each other's Ethel

so, when I texted what she knew
 was the end but never said
she came
on a cold dark January night
with bananas, wine, toilet paper & a jug of water

she came with provisions

because
the Ethels had been to war before
and together, had persevered

seeing her through the glass
made my reflection stronger
as my eyes blended with hers
they no longer cried
no longer looked empty

no longer looked
alone
because,
even though I could not hug
could not touch
we were what we had always been
what all of us had always been
—connected

## Acknowledgments

*you died, the mail* Door Is A Jar fall issue 2021
*fishing with corn, the ladder*, OpenDoor Magazine June 2021 July 2021 anthology

Made in the USA
Columbia, SC
10 February 2024